D1506071

The Surrender at Yorktown

CORNERSTONES OF FREEDOM™

SECOND SERIES

Melissa Whitcraft

Children's Press®
A Division of Scholastic Inc.
New York • Toronto • London • Auckland • Sydney
Mexico City • New Delhi • Hong Kong
Danbury, Connecticut

Photographs ©2004: Art Resource, NY: 20 bottom, 45 bottom right (Giraudon), 3 (Reunion des Musees Nationaux), 38, 45 bottom left (The New York Public Library); Bridgeman Art Library International Ltd., London/New York/Lauros/Giraudon: 33; Corbis Images: cover bottom, 8, 23, 24, 36 (Bettmann), 4, 27, 29, 30, 39, 45 top left; Hulton|Archive/Getty Images: 14, 18, 20 top, 28, 44 bottom; Independence National Historical Park via SODA: 26; Library of Congress: 15; National Portrait Gallery, London: 10; North Wind Picture Archives: 5, 6, 7, 9, 11 left, 11 right, 12, 13, 16, 17, 21, 35, 37, 44 center, 45 top right; Stock Montage, Inc.: 19, 22, 25, 32, 44 top; The State Museum of Pennsylvania/Pennsylvania Historical & Museum Commission via SODA: 40; U.S. Capitol Historical Society via SODA: cover top (National Geographic), 41.

Library of Congress Cataloging-in-Publication Data

Whitcraft, Melissa.

The Surrender at Yorktown / Melissa Whitcraft.

p. cm. — (Cornerstones of freedom. Second series)

Summary: Details events that led to the Declaration of Independence and Revolutionary War, looks at major battles including the Battle of Yorktown, and reviews the formation of a United States government. Includes bibliographical references and index.

ISBN 0-516-24234-2

1. United States—History—Revolution, 1775–1783—Juvenile literature. 2. Yorktown (Va.)—History—Siege, 1781—Juvenile literature. 3. United States—Politics and government—1775–1783—Juvenile literature. [1. United States—History—Revolution, 1775–1783—Campaigns. 2. Yorktown (Va.)—History—Siege, 1781. 3. United States—Politics and government—1775–1783.] I. Title. II. Series.

E208.W49 2004

973.3'37—dc21

2003011244

1 2 3 4 5 6 7 8 9 10 R 13 12 11 10 09 08 07 06 05 04

At noon on October 19, 1781, two armies, stretching out over a mile, stood at attention on either side of a dirt road leading into the small tobacco port of Yorktown, Virginia. The American Continental Army was under the command of General George Washington. The other army was French, led by the Comte de Rochambeau. France was helping the Americans fight their war against England. Dr. James Thacher, who served with the Continentals, said, "The French troops, in complete uniform, displayed a martial and noble appearance . . . The Americans, though not all in uniforms, exhibited an erect, soldierly air, and every [face] beamed with satisfaction and joy." Together, the two armies waited for the British army to appear.

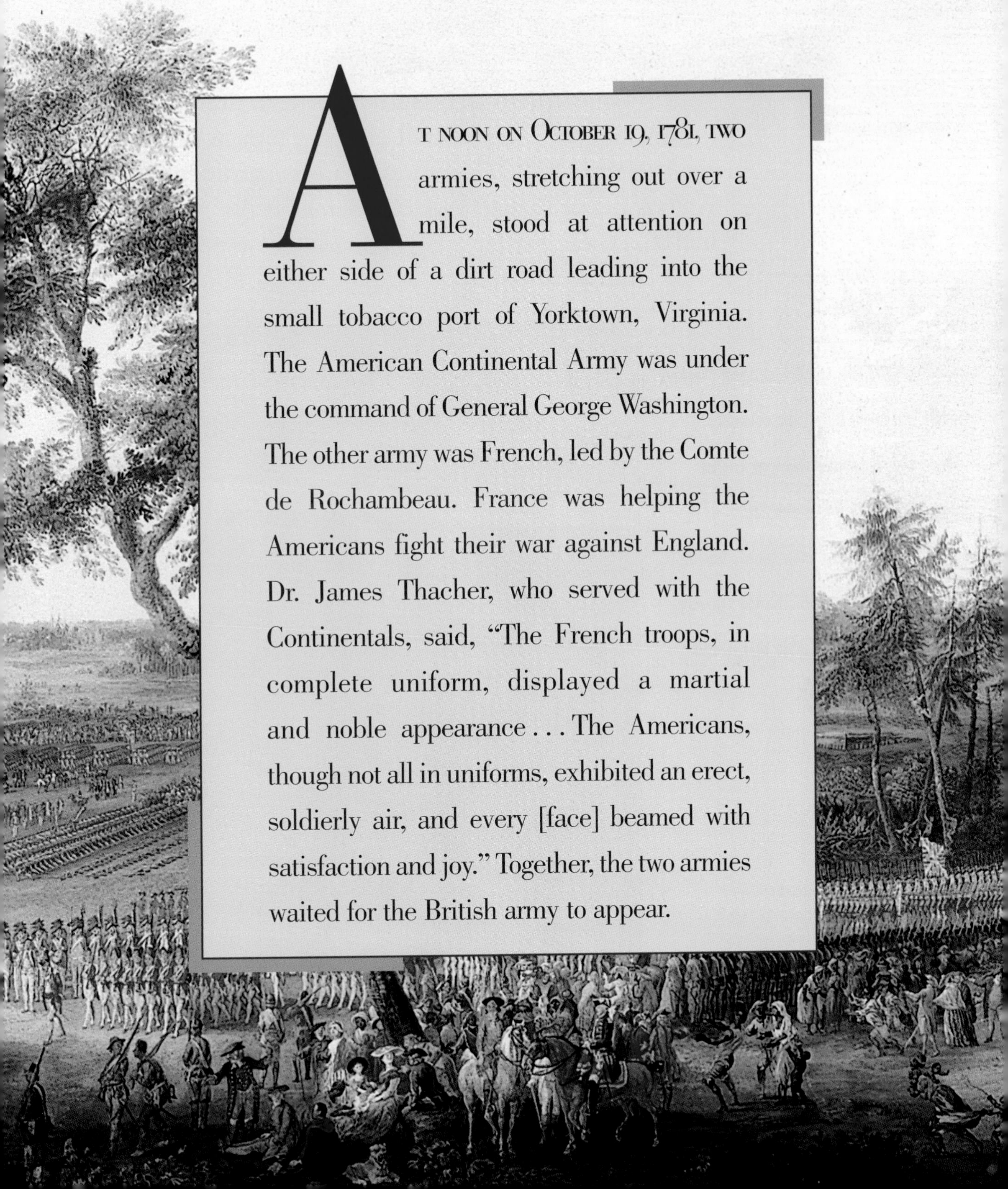

Two hours later, British troops marched out of Yorktown "in a slow and solemn step." When they saw the French, the British thought they were surrendering to the French. However, when the French band played "Yankee Doodle," they realized the truth: The British were surrendering to the Americans. The colonists had defeated the mighty British and won their war for independence.

"YANKEE DOODLE"

In the colonial era, the British sang "Yankee Doodle" to make fun of the colonists. A *yankee* was an uneducated New England farmer; a *doodle* was a simpleton, or someone without common sense. During the Revolution, Americans turned "Yankee Doodle" into a song of pride that is still popular today.

This famous painting by A.M. Willard is called "The Spirit of '76" or "Yankee Doodle." The fife player, drummer, and minuteman represent the independent spirit of the colonies during the Revolutionary War.

New England colonists stroll through town in the late 1600s.

THE THIRTEEN COLONIES

After the founding of Jamestown in 1607, England established thirteen **colonies** along the eastern coast of North America. The Atlantic Ocean separated these communities from their native country. However, because they were colonies, the settlements were still part of England. Connected through their shared heritage, the two were also tied together by their mutual interest in trade.

The colonists sent England valuable natural resources, raw materials that could be traded or made into manufactured goods. They supplied British **merchants** with codfish caught off Cape Cod, Massachusetts, and timber cut from America's

Even in 1667, New Amsterdam (now Manhattan) was a busy economic center. Large boats, which could easily reach it from the Hudson River, carried food, timber, and tobacco, among other things.

forests. They also sent beaver pelts. Beaver fur, popular throughout Europe, was made into men's hats and winter coats. Rice and tobacco from the Carolina colonies were also **exported** because these crops did not grow in England.

While much of their trade was with England, colonial merchants also sent American goods throughout the world. Colonial ships sailed to Europe, the Caribbean, the Far

East, and Africa. In addition, the colonies **imported** goods such as sugar, molasses, cloth, and tea from countries other than England. Some merchants also brought African slaves to America.

During this period, colonial ports were busy centers for exporting and importing a variety of goods. As a result,

The first people to arrive in America from England created thirteen colonies along the eastern seaboard. People came for many different reasons such as religious freedom and to search for riches.

THE THIRTEEN COLONIES

The thirteen original colonies were Georgia, New Hampshire, Massachusetts, Rhode Island, Connecticut, New York, New Jersey, Pennsylvania, Delaware, Maryland, Virginia, North Carolina, and South Carolina. Until the American Revolution, most colonists considered themselves part of the British Empire.

merchants on both sides of the Atlantic Ocean made money, and the colonists were content to be part of England.

The early colonists were also satisfied with their relationship with England because, for the most part, England left them alone to run their colonies as they wished. In 1619, for instance, Virginia created the first colonial **legislature** in America, the Virginia House of Burgesses. The twenty-two representatives in the legislature were elected citizens, or burgesses, who came from eleven different sections of the colony.

Even though they were ultimately ruled by England, each of the colonies created their own governing documents, such as this colonial constitution of Pennsylvania, dated 1682.

PENNSYLVANIA: A PRIMER. 75

The FRAME of the
GOVERNMENT
OF THE
Province of Pennsilvania
IN
AMERICA:
Together with certain
LAWS
Agreed upon in England
BY THE
GOVERNOUR
AND
Divers FREE-MEN of the aforesaid
PROVINCE.

To be further Explained and Confirmed there by the first *Provincial Council* and *General Assembly* that shall be held, if they see meet.

Printed in the Year MDCLXXXII.

FAC-SIMILE OF TITLE PAGE OF PENN'S "FRAME OF GOVERNMENT, 1682."

Even though the British governor of Virginia sometimes vetoed, or rejected, a law the burgesses passed, the colonists still had a voice. They elected their own representatives, wrote their own laws, and passed their own taxes. These taxes required individuals to give a certain amount of money—a tax—to the colony to help it meet its expenses.

By the mid-seventeenth century, England's attitude toward the colonies changed. Between 1651 and 1673, **Parliament** passed the Navigation Acts. These laws demanded that all goods exported from or imported to the colonies be carried on either British or colonial ships. The acts also stated that if the colonies wanted to

Colonists kept track of shipping laws and taxes in the counting room.

trade with other nations such as France or Holland, their goods had to be sold to British merchants first.

In addition, colonists were forced to sell all their tobacco, sugar, and cotton to England. Finally, to be sure that England had a market for its manufactured goods, Parliament refused to allow the colonies to export manufactured goods of their own. The colonists now had no market for their woven woolen garments, hats, or iron tools.

This policy, called colonial mercantilism, brought additional income and trade into England and made sure that the colonial merchants would have a market for their raw materials. However, because they were no longer allowed to trade throughout the world, the colonial merchants started to resent England's power over them. In the end, England's American trade policies would backfire in ways Parliament never anticipated.

THE MOLASSES ACT OF 1733

The Molasses Act of 1733 was another example of how England attempted to control colonial trade. This act placed a heavy duty, or tax, on any sugar, molasses, or rum that Americans imported from French merchants in the Caribbean. Parliament demanded a tax on these French goods because England wanted its colonial merchants to support British sugar plantation owners in the Caribbean.

TENSIONS RISE

After the French and Indian War (1756–1763), England became even more demanding. At the end of the conflict, England controlled most of the territory in North America. However, the war against France and its Native American allies had cost a great deal. England was in debt. To raise much-needed income, the English king, George III, taxed the colonies every chance he got.

In a stubborn show of power, King George III would push colonists to the breaking point with strict tax laws and harsh punishments.

In 1764, Parliament passed the Revenue, or Sugar Act. Replacing the Molasses Act, the Sugar Act taxed imported molasses, fabric, dye, coffee, and wines. The Quartering Act of 1765 made the colonies pay for housing British troops. In 1765, Parliament also passed the Stamp Act. The Stamp Act taxed all printed materials.

The Stamp Act pushed many colonists over the edge. It was the first act to demand that all money raised be sent to England. In Philadelphia, people rioted. In Boston, a mob burned down the house of a British judge. In October, representatives from nine colonies held a Stamp Act **Congress** in New York. There they wrote a document saying no taxes could be imposed on a colony unless those taxes were passed by the colony's own legislature.

To calm the colonists, Parliament withdrew the Stamp Act. However, in 1767, Parliament wrote the Townshend Acts, which demanded that the colonies pay a tax on all glass, lead, tea, paper, and paint imported from England. Once more, there was an outcry. Mercy Otis Warren, a

These are some of the British stamps issued under the Stamp Act. Stamps were to be placed on newspapers, shipping bills, legal papers, and other official documents.

People throughout the colonies rioted against the Stamp Act.

Mercy Otis Warren wrote a history of the Revolutionary War that is still considered important for its factual information.

patriotic poet and playwright, encouraged women to **boycott** all British goods. She considered this a "small sacrifice."

On March 5, 1770, tension between the British and Americans spilled over. That night, a group of townspeople in Boston started teasing a British soldier. Nine soldiers came to his aid. A shot was fired. More shots followed, and five colonists were killed.

Patriots throughout America were outraged by what became known as "the Boston Massacre." Newspapers carried angry articles. Church ministers delivered sermons with titles such as "Innocent Blood Crying from the Streets of Boston."

As a result, Parliament repealed the Townshend Acts, but kept the tax on tea. This insult proved too much for colonial tea merchants. When three British ships loaded with tea arrived in Boston Harbor in November 1773, American dockworkers refused to unload them. On December 16, approximately 7,000 people came out to protest the tax. That night, Patriots disguised as Mohawk Indians boarded the ships and dumped 342 chests of tea into the water.

When King George heard about the "tea party," he said, "The die is now cast . . . The colonies must either submit or triumph." To make them submit, Parliament closed Boston

When three ships filled with tea arrived in Boston Harbor, the colonists demanded the ships return to London. When the owner refused, a group of colonists dressed as Indians dumped the tea into the harbor.

Harbor and put a strict military governor in charge of Massachusetts. These Intolerable Acts made the colonists even angrier. As George Washington said, "The cause of Boston is the cause of America."

"GIVE ME LIBERTY!"

Patrick Henry, a patriotic representative in the House of Burgesses, agreed with Washington's sentiments. On March 23, 1775, he gave a passionate speech that convinced the legislature to create a Virginia **militia** to protect the colony from British troops. In part, Henry said, ". . . war is inevitable . . . Our [brothers in Boston] are already in the

THE FIRST CONTINENTAL CONGRESS

The First Continental Congress met in Philadelphia from September 5 to October 26, 1774. Delegates from twelve colonies came to protest England's unfair tax practices. John Adams said that the men present were "a collection of the greatest men upon this continent."

Members of the First Continental Congress met in Philadephia to define American rights and create a plan of resistance.

Patrick Henry's skills as an orator, or speaker, made him a leader in many protests against the British.

field! Why stand we here idle? . . . I know not what course others may take; but as for me, give me liberty, or give me death."

Henry's passion was felt by many colonists who were frustrated by England's trade and tax policies. However, these frustrations were not the only reasons Americans struggled under British rule. New political ideas were taking hold in the eighteenth century—ideas that centered on

British troops march through Boston.

the radical notion that ordinary people, not kings, had the right to govern countries.

The American colonists understood these ideas. In town meetings and colonial legislatures, people from all levels of society came together to run the colony. Farmers and craftsmen voted with merchants and ministers. This experience showed the colonists that a government run by the people worked. They did not need a king or his Parliament to tell them what to do.

Finally, on April 19, 1775, the "inevitable" war Henry had warned about began. That morning,

THE MIDNIGHT RIDE

On the night of April 18, 1775, Paul Revere, William Dawes, and Dr. Samuel Prescott rode out of Boston to warn the Patriots that the British were coming to Lexington and Concord. Revere and Dawes were captured by the British; only Prescott made it as far as Concord.

On his famous ride to Lexington, Massachusetts, Paul Revere shouted warnings to homeowners along the way.

General Thomas Gage, the governor of Massachusetts, marched out of Boston into the small village of Lexington with seven hundred British soldiers. He was on his way to Concord to destroy American ammunition and weapons there. He also hoped to arrest Patriot leaders Samuel Adams and John Hancock.

At Lexington, Gage was met by John Parker and about seventy of his **minutemen**. Realizing he was outnumbered, Parker ordered his men to leave. Before they could, someone fired a shot.

No one knows who fired first, but as American poet Ralph Waldo Emerson wrote, "It was the shot heard 'round the world." The colonies would lose eight minutemen at Lexington. They would lose more when Gage marched into Concord, and still more as the British retreated back to Boston. King George III had his answer: Many lives would be lost, but the

On April 19, 1775, minutemen faced British soldiers on Lexington Common in the first battle of the American Revolution.

A minuteman—a soldier prepared to turn out for war at a minute's notice—gets ready to join the battle.

colonists would not submit. They had had enough of trade restrictions, taxes, and kings. The colonists would fight. They would take liberty or death.

WAR

The day after Lexington and Concord, thousands of New England Patriots answered the call to arms. Militiamen from Massachusetts, New Hampshire, and Connecticut surrounded Boston. For the moment, the city was under **siege** and the British army was contained.

Representatives of the Second Continental Congress met in Philadelphia's State House, later named Independence Hall.

A skilled leader, George Washington was unanimously elected to lead the Continental Army.

By May 1775, the New England militia outside Boston needed more soldiers and supplies. Decisions had to be made. Delegates from all thirteen colonies met in Philadelphia on May 10 at the Second Continental Congress.

The Second Continental Congress became the government for the colonies during the war. One of the first actions the Congress took was to create the Continental Army. The delegates chose George Washington as commander-in-chief. Washington had been in the French and Indian War and served in the House of Burgesses. John Adams, a delegate from Massachusetts, said Washington's "greatest talents and universal character would . . . unite . . . the Colonies better than any other person alive."

For the next six years, American and British armies faced each other across rolling fields and narrow city streets. They fought in the heat of summer and the cold of winter. Professional soldiers, the British troops were well disciplined and well equipped. Most of the Americans had no military experience. They were farmers, shopkeepers, landowners, and merchants making do with few supplies.

While many American soldiers were members of the Continental Army and wore blue and white uniforms, others were members of small, local militia units. These men fought together, usually to protect their farms or settlements.

Some soldiers fought because they believed in the colonies' right to independence. Others joined because Congress promised them land or money for their services. Still others were drafted, or recruited. Many of the officers had similar backgrounds to George Washington. They were plantation owners, landlords, and merchants; men who had held positions of authority in their community.

A few women fought with the Continentals. Some came to help their husbands. Another, Deborah Samson, disguised as a man, fought for more than a year. African Americans, both free and enslaved, fought for both the British and the Americans. Crispus Attucks, a Patriot who was part African and part Native American, was killed in the Boston Massacre. For the most part, however, Native Americans supported England. They hoped a British victory would keep the colonists from moving farther west onto their lands.

Mary Hays McCauly (or Mary Ludwig Hays) earned the nickname Molly Pitcher because she brought pitchers of water to the exhausted men fighting the Battle of Monmouth. Her many heroic actions that day guaranteed her an important place in history.

The war did not go well for the Americans in the beginning. The troops were undisciplined. The army lacked supplies. Washington was saved from surrendering in late 1776 because merchant Robert Morris used his worldwide contacts to raise much-needed money. The additional funds bought tons of gunpowder and other war materials, but still the army struggled.

Even though there were dark periods when it looked as though all was lost, the colonists did not give up. Often they were inspired by the writings of Thomas Paine. In January 1776, he published a fifty-page booklet entitled *Common Sense*. This small book encouraged the colonies to fight because England had imprisoned them with its taxes and trade restrictions. More important, *Common Sense* explained that "a government of our own [was] our natural right."

The booklet was so popular that by March, more than 100,000 copies were sold. Washington believed that Paine's words "[worked] a powerful change in the minds of many men" to bring colonists firmly onto the Patriots' side.

Thomas Paine's writing inspired the colonists. His work, *Common Sense*, was read and debated by Americans everywhere.

On December 19, 1777, Washington took his troops to Valley Forge, Pennsylvania, to wait out the winter. The situation looked bleak. The British army still controlled New York as they had since Washington fled the city in September 1776. The Americans had won the Battle of Saratoga, New York, in October 1777, but they had lost at Brandywine and Germantown, Pennsylvania. Worse, the British had also taken Philadelphia, forcing the Continental Congress to escape to York, Pennsylvania.

THE DECLARATION OF INDEPENDENCE

While the army fought, delegates at the Second Continental Congress asked Thomas Jefferson, a delegate from Virginia, to draft a document proclaiming that the thirteen colonies were now free of England. Jefferson said that the document, called the Declaration of Independence, was "an expression of the American mind." Finished on July 4, 1776, it states the American belief that all people are created equal and that the government is the servant of the people.

Along with John Adams and Benjamin Franklin, Thomas Jefferson was one of the most important leaders of the Revolution. He would later become the third president of the country.

The winter was rough. The soldiers were cold and hungry. Their clothes were in rags. Many walked through the snow without shoes. With no housing, they built 16-by-14 foot (4.9 by-4.3 m) huts for twelve men to share. Of the 12,000 at Valley Forge, 2,000 died from illness. Others deserted.

Yet, out of this disastrous situation, an army was built. Washington walked among the troops to encourage them. His wife, Martha, nursed the sick. Baron Friedrich von Steuben, a German drillmaster, taught the soldiers military discipline and important fighting skills. He also demanded they take pride in themselves and their cause.

The soldiers of the Continental Army endured many hardships during the winter of 1777–1778 at Valley Forge. Despite this, however, Washington and his generals managed to build a stronger military unit.

★ ★ ★ ★

THE MARQUIS DE LAFAYETTE (1757–1834)

Of all the Europeans who helped the Americans, Lafayette was the most famous. A member of the French nobility, Lafayette believed in the principles of a democratic government. He was also a close friend and aide to Washington and earned the respect of American generals and soldiers alike. A hero of the Revolution, Lafayette was remembered even many years later. In 1917, when American troops landed in France to help the French during World War I, their slogan was, "Lafayette, we are here."

Marquis de Lafayette's strong support for the American cause made him a valuable officer in the Continental Army.

In spring, the army received much-needed supplies. Finally, the soldiers had enough clothing and food to regain their strength. New recruits also arrived, and in May Washington found out that France had joined the war as America's ally. Overjoyed, Washington said he was thankful that "a powerful friend" had risen up to help the Americans "establish [their] Liberty and Independence."

France helped the Americans because they knew England would lose power in Europe if it lost the colonies. The French also hoped to become America's trading partner. The partnership would help France recover its losses in the

French troops, as well as additional supplies from France, arrived in Rhode Island to help the Americans.

French and Indian War. When France's ally, Spain, also entered the war in 1779, England's conflict with the colonies became a world war over trade.

THE WAR IN THE SOUTH

The training at Valley Forge turned the Continental soldiers into an army that could stand up to the disciplined British forces. However, the battles were not easily won. In the south, the British captured Savannah, Georgia, in 1778 and Charleston, South Carolina, in 1780. Then, British General Henry Clinton turned Charleston over to Major General Charles Cornwallis while he returned north. Despite Cornwallis's belief that the war had to be won in the south, Clinton was convinced that the French fleet was going to attack New York City.

Major General Charles Cornwallis was instrumental in many British victories during the Revolution.

NATHANAEL GREENE (1742–1786)

Nathanael Greene (left), born into a Rhode Island business family, joined the Rhode Island Militia soon after Lexington and Concord. As Quartermaster at Valley Forge, he was responsible for resupplying Washington's troops. Made the Commander of the Southern Army, Greene fought in the Carolinas until the end of the war.

On December 2, 1780, Washington sent General Nathanael Greene to Charlotte, North Carolina, to take over the American troops stationed there. Greene divided the soldiers into two groups. One, led by Brigadier General Daniel Morgan was, as Greene said, "to give protection" and lift the spirit of the American Patriots in the area. Greene planned to turn the other soldiers into a disciplined

The Continental Army's victory at the Battle of Cowpens was an important turning point in the war.

military force to face Cornwallis. By separating his soldiers into two groups, Greene was forcing Cornwallis to fight on two fronts.

Greene also knew how to use his local militiamen. They knew the surrounding countryside, and were, as a British officer described them, "the most hardy warlike people in America." They lured the British into the woods or up the mountains and attacked. Then they moved on before the British could catch them. This tactic, called guerilla warfare, worked well against the British, who were unfamiliar with the landscape.

On January 17, 1781, Cornwallis sent Lieutenant Colonel Tarleton to fight Morgan at the Battle of Cowpens, North

Carolina. Despite having more men, Tarleton was defeated. Afterward, Morgan rejoined Greene and together they headed back into Virginia.

Cornwallis raced after Greene. He wanted to fight the American general before Greene was fully prepared. For six weeks, Greene led Cornwallis through North Carolina, forcing the British general to make mistakes. To keep moving as fast as he could, Cornwallis did not wait for the slow soldiers to catch up. He also allowed his main force to get farther and farther ahead of their supplies.

Once Cornwallis reached the Dan River, which separated North Carolina and Virginia, he had to stop. Greene had arranged for boats, but Cornwallis had no way to get across. Disappointed, he turned south to resupply his army and wait for Greene's return.

In March, Greene recrossed the Dan. On the fifteenth, he and Cornwallis met at the Battle of Guilford Courthouse in North Carolina. Greene had approximately 4,000 soldiers. Cornwallis only had 2,000, and suffered terrible losses.

To save his men from a British artillery, or large gun, attack, Greene retreated. To recover, Cornwallis moved his men back into Virginia. In August, he set up base in Yorktown. On the York River, close to the Chesapeake Bay, Cornwallis thought it was only a matter of time before General Clinton arrived from New York with more men and supplies. Expressing how exhausted he was, Cornwallis wrote to a friend, "I am quite tired of marching about the country in quest of adventures."

WASHINGTON COMES SOUTH

While Cornwallis waited for supplies and built fortifications in the heat of August, Washington met the French General Comte de Rochambeau in Rhode Island. Washington had thought that the French and American armies should attack New York. Rochambeau, however, convinced the American general that the city was too well protected.

Washington and Rochambeau joined American and French forces to battle the British.

Together, Washington and Rochambeau moved their armies hundreds of miles toward Yorktown. The path they followed is now considered one of the most historically important routes in American history.

Then word came from the French General Lafayette, who was in Virginia, that Cornwallis was in Yorktown. In addition, Rochambeau and Washington heard from Comte de Grasse, the admiral of the French fleet. He informed them that his fleet would get to the Chesapeake Bay by mid-September. The catch was that he could only stay one month before the stormy fall weather forced him back to the West Indies.

With Cornwallis in Yorktown and the French fleet controlling the Chesapeake, Washington and Rochambeau knew they had a chance. It was a slim one, but if they could get to Yorktown before de Grasse left, they might be able to capture Cornwallis. With a plan in place, they headed for Virginia.

In eighteenth-century America, moving two armies 500 miles (805 kilometers) was not easy. There were very few, if any, bridges over the rivers. Most roads were only rough trails. Quickly transporting two armies that spoke two different languages was even more difficult. However, that is exactly what Washington and Rochambeau did. On August 19, 7,000 French and American soldiers started south.

Washington left about 2,500 men in New Jersey, across the Hudson River from New York City. He had them make noise and set up campfires. He wanted the British to think the entire army was there preparing for battle so that he could get away without being followed. By September 2, Clinton realized Washington was on his way south. Quickly, he sent word to Cornwallis.

AMERICANS AT SEA

The Americans did not have a very large navy. They depended on their allies. However, American naval captain John Paul Jones showed the same spirit at sea that his countrymen showed on land. In September 1779, in a battle off the coast of England, Jones's ship, the *Bonhomme Richard*, defeated the better-equipped British battleship, the *Serapis*.

As the French and American armies continued south, averaging about 15 miles (24.14 km) per day, de Grasse's fleet of twenty-three ships, carrying 3,000 additional soldiers, reached the Chesapeake Bay. Arriving earlier than expected and joined by additional French ships from Rhode Island, de Grasse surprised the British Admiral Graves. After a series of battles that lasted from September 5 to September 9, Graves withdrew and headed back to New York. The French now controlled the Chesapeake Bay. The British at Yorktown could no longer expect reinforcements by sea. Even if Clinton arrived with the fleet, the French would never let him through to the York River. Cornwallis was cut off.

The British warship *Sharon* was destroyed in battle at Chesapeake Bay.

THE SIEGE OF YORKTOWN

On September 28 outside of Yorktown, Washington and Rochambeau met up with Lafayette, Baron von Steuben, American general Anthony Wayne, and their men. The Americans now had 9,000 soldiers, and the French had

7,800. This force of 16,800 was ready to meet Cornwallis's 8,000. As the armies moved to within 2 miles (3.2 km) of Yorktown, British soldiers heard the American soldiers, with their horses and wagons. The enemy had arrived.

The siege began on October 6. The combined French and American armies surrounded Yorktown and prepared to attack from the southwest. They built protective trenches and set up

Washington fired the first cannon at Yorktown on October 9, 1781. American and French soldiers would continue to shower Yorktown with cannonfire for days.

their artillery. The French, under Rochambeau, came in from the northwest. The Americans, under Washington and Lafayette, approached from the northeast.

On October 9, the American bombardment began. By October 10, the forty-six guns in place were causing so much damage that it was difficult for Cornwallis's troops to return fire. By October 14, the two armies were close enough to attack. Alexander Hamilton led 400 men against one of the British fortifications. Other French and American troops attacked other points along the British defense. British soldiers tried to dismantle some of the guns, but they were driven back.

On the evening of October 16, Cornwallis attempted to cross the York River. He hoped to fight his way free from there. However, a storm kept him and his men from getting across.

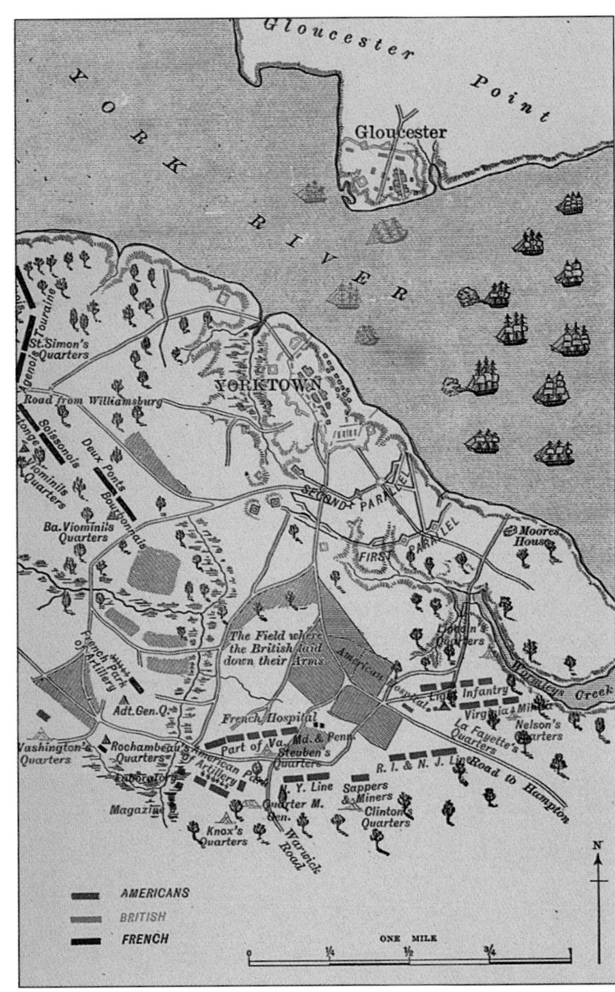

This map of Yorktown shows the main areas of battle outlined in red, including the York River, which Cornwallis had hoped to cross and lead his troops to safety.

By the next morning, October 17, the allies had one hundred guns ready. Cornwallis realized all his defenses were about to be destroyed. Surrounded, outgunned, short of food and ammunition, and with many soldiers wounded and sick, Cornwallis knew it was over. A British drummer boy stood at the top of a trench and beat his drum. An officer stood next to him waving a white handkerchief. The battle was over. The Continentals had won.

American soldiers cheered. Washington told them to be silent. “Let history [cheer] for you,” he said. The general knew that it was too early to know what this victory meant. Only history would tell.

In an act that symbolized the British defeat at Yorktown, Major General Cornwallis's sword was handed over to the Americans.

For the next two days, Cornwallis and Washington worked out the terms of surrender. Cornwallis's entire army would surrender along with all their artillery. Officers could return to England or go to British-occupied American port cities. Officers would also be allowed to keep their side arms, or small guns.

The soldiers could keep their personal belongings, but all would be marched to internment camps in Virginia, Maryland, and Pennsylvania. Washington also added, “I expect the Sick and Wounded will be supplied with their own Hospital Stores [medicines and bandages] and be attended by [their own British doctors].”

THE WORLD TURNED UPSIDE DOWN

Some historians say that “The World Turned Upside Down” wasn't written until fifty years after the surrender. However, the song describes ponies riding men, grass eating cows, and mice chasing cats. It certainly expresses how strange the world must have seemed to the British on October 19, 1781.

On October 19, Cornwallis's 8,000 men marched out of Yorktown, playing a song called, “The World Turned Upside Down.” As Dr. Thacher, the Continental Army doctor, described the event, there were a few thousand “spectators from the country” watching, “but universal silence and order prevailed.”

Cornwallis didn't come. Saying he was ill, he sent his second in command, Brigadier General Charles O'Hara. O'Hara started to surrender to Rochambeau, who refused and pointed to Washington. Washington also refused and made O'Hara surrender to his second in command, Major General Benjamin Lincoln. When the troops gave up their weapons, Washington was not in the field. "The Great American Commander," as Dr. Thacher called him, "mounted on his noble [horse]" and, surrounded by his aides, stood off to the side.

General Clinton showed up on October 24. His fleet brought 7,000 reinforcements, but de Grasse's ships sent the British back to New York. Clinton was too late.

Washington had only defeated one fourth of the British Army. However, Parliament believed that the victory meant that England would eventually lose the colonies. At this point, the war was taking too long and costing too much money. It was time for peace.

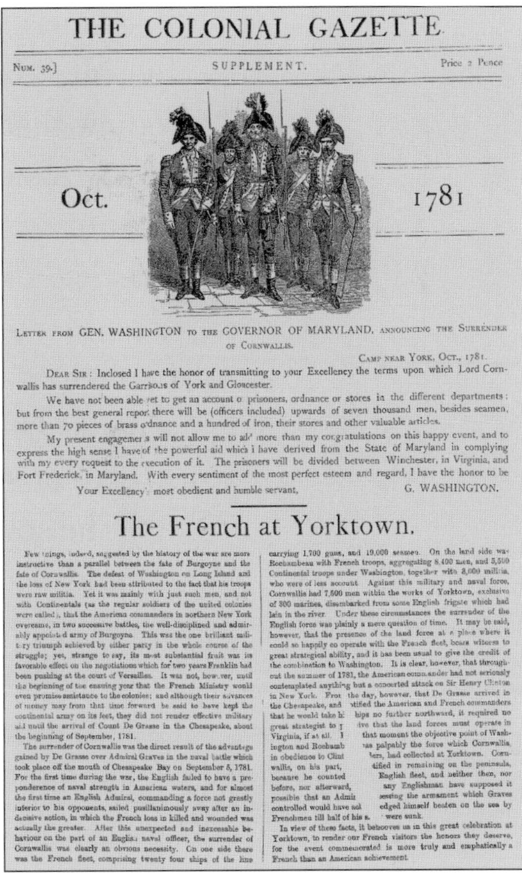

THE COLONIAL GAZETTE

NUM. 39.] SUPPLEMENT. Price 2 Pence

Oct. 1781

LETTER FROM GEN. WASHINGTON TO THE GOVERNOR OF MARYLAND, ANNOUNCING THE SURRENDER OF CORNWALLIS.

CAMP NEAR YORK, OCT., 1781.

DEAR SIR: Inclosed I have the honor of transmitting to your Excellency the terms upon which Lord Cornwallis has surrendered the Garrisons of York and Gloucester.

We have not been able yet to get an account of prisoners, ordnance or stores in the different departments: but from the best general report there will be (officers included) upwards of seven thousand men, besides seamen, more than 70 pieces of brass ordnance and a hundred of iron, their stores and other valuable articles.

My present engagements will not allow me to add more than my congratulations on this happy event, and to express the high sense I have of the powerful aid which I have derived from the State of Maryland in complying with my every request to the execution of it. The prisoners will be divided between Winchester, in Virginia, and Fort Frederick, in Maryland. With every sentiment of the most perfect esteem and regard, I have the honor to be

Your Excellency's most obedient and humble servant,

G. WASHINGTON.

The French at Yorktown.

Few things, indeed, suggested by the history of the war are more instructive than a parallel between the fate of Burgoyne and the fate of Cornwallis. The defeat of Washington on Long Island and the loss of New York had been attributed to the fact that his troops were raw militia. Yet it was mainly with just such men, and not with Continentals (as the regular soldiers of the united colonies were called), that the American commanders in northern New York overcame, in two successive battles, the well-disciplined and admirably appointed army of Burgoyne. This was the one brilliant military triumph achieved by either party in the whole course of the struggle; yet, strange to say, its most substantial fruit was its favorable effect on the negotiations which for two years Franklin had been pushing at the court of Versailles. It was not, however, until the beginning of the ensuing year that the French Ministry would even promise assistance to the colonies; and although their advances of money may from that time forward be said to have kept the continental army on its feet, they did not render effective military aid until the arrival of Count De Grasse in the Chesapeake, about the beginning of September, 1781.

The surrender of Cornwallis was the direct result of the advantage gained by De Grasse over Admiral Graves in the naval battle which took place off the mouth of Chesapeake Bay on September 5, 1781. For the first time during the war, the English failed to have a preponderence of naval strength in American waters, and for almost the first time an English Admiral, commanding a force not greatly inferior to his opponents, sailed pusillanimously away after an indecisive action, in which the French loss in killed and wounded was actually the greater. After this unexpected and inexcusable behaviour on the part of an English naval officer, the surrender of Cornwallis was clearly an obvious necessity. On one side there was the French fleet, comprising twenty four ships of the line carrying 1,700 guns, and 19,000 seamen. On the land side was Rochambeau with French troops, aggregating 8,400 men, and 5,500 Continental troops under Washington, together with 3,000 militia, who were of less account. Against this military and naval force, Cornwallis had 7,500 men within the works of Yorktown, exclusive of 800 marines, disembarked from some English frigate which had lain in the river. Under these circumstances the surrender of the English force was plainly a mere question of time. It may be said, however, that the presence of the land force at a place where it could so happily co operate with the French fleet, bears witness to great strategical ability, and it has been usual to give the credit of the combination to Washington. It is clear, however, that throughout the summer of 1781, the American commander had not seriously contemplated anything but a concerted attack on Sir Henry Clinton in New York. Fro[illegible] the day, however, that De Grasse arrived in the Chesapeake, and [illegible]tified the American and French commanders that he would take hi[illegible]hips no further northward, it required no great strategist to [illegible]ive that the land forces must operate in Virginia, if at all. [illegible] that moment the objective point of Washington and Rochamb[illegible]as palpably the force which Cornwallis, in obedience to Clint[illegible]ders, had collected at Yorktown. Cornwallis, on his part, [illegible]tified in remaining on the peninsula, because he counted [illegible] English fleet, and neither then, nor before, nor afterward, [illegible] any Englishman have supposed it possible that an Admir[illegible]sessing the armament which Graves controlled would have ack[illegible]edged himself beaten on the sea by Frenchmen till half of his s[illegible] were sunk.

In view of these facts, it behooves us in this great celebration at Yorktown, to render our French visitors the honors they deserve, for the event commemorated is more truly and emphatically a French than an American achievement.

***The Colonial Gazette* printed a letter from General Washington to the Governor of Maryland announcing the surrender of Cornwallis.**

THE UNITED STATES OF AMERICA

In September 1783, the Treaty of Paris was signed, officially ending the war. American representatives in Paris included Benjamin Franklin and John Adams. The treaty granted the colonies independence from England. It also gave the new country borders that reached from the Atlantic Ocean west to the Mississippi River and south from the Great Lakes to the northern border of Spanish Florida.

Both countries had the right to use the Mississippi River. In addition, the Americans agreed to ask the state legislatures to allow **Loyalists** to keep their property.

Most likely, these gestures were made to encourage both trade and friendship with England. As Franklin said, once the treaty was signed, "We are all friends with England and all Mankind. May we never see another war . . . for in my opinion, there never was a good war or a bad peace."

Independence secured, the new country now had to create a government. In May 1787, fifty-five delegates met in Philadelphia for the Constitutional Convention. Just as the colonies had come together to decide their fate with England, the thirteen states came together now to decide their fate as a new nation.

After months of discussion, debate, and **compromise**, the delegates had a government. It was divided into three branches. The executive branch was the office of the elected president. One of the president's jobs would be to approve or reject laws. The legislative branch, Congress, would write the laws and taxes. Finally, the judicial branch, including the Supreme Court and other federal courts, would interpret the laws.

The Constitutional Convention of 1787, presided over by George Washington, resulted in the writing of the U.S. Constitution.

Thirty-nine delegates signed the Constitution. Only three delegates—two from Virginia and one from Massachusetts—refused to sign the document.

On September 17, 1787, delegates signed the Constitution. When Benjamin Franklin walked outside, he was asked what kind of government the country had, "A **republic**," he replied. "If you can keep it."

Some of the newly formed states accepted the Constitution immediately. Others didn't. There was nothing in the document that explained the rights citizens had fought for. Once the delegates agreed to add these changes, called the Bill of Rights, all state legislatures signed. Over time, more amendments would be added.

On April 30, 1789, in New York City, George Washington, wearing an American-made brown suit, was sworn in as the country's first president. John Adams was vice president. The thirteen colonies were now the United States of America. Frustration over trade resulted in a government run by the people, for the people. A great experiment in democracy was about to begin.

Glossary

boycott—to refuse to buy goods as an act of protest

colonies—communities of people living in a territory separated from their native country, but still tied politically and economically to the country

compromise—a method of reaching an agreement in which each side gives up something that it wants

congress—an assembly of representatives who meet to discuss problems or issues

delegates—people who act as representatives on behalf of others

exported—sent from one country to another in exchange for goods, money, or services

imported—brought into a country from overseas

legislature—an elected body of people responsible for making the laws of a state or nation

Loyalists—people who supported England during the Revolution

merchants—people who buy and sell goods; traders

militia—a local army of ordinary citizens not attached to a regular army

minutemen—name given to colonial militias in New England who were ready to fight in a minute

Parliament—the governmental body in England that makes the laws

Patriots—people who supported independence and were willing to fight for it

republic—a government whose citizens are responsible for electing representatives to run the country

siege—the surrounding of a city or town by an opposing army

Timeline: The Surrender

1651–1673	1733	1756–1763	1764	1765
Parliament passes the Navigation Acts.	Parliament passes the Molasses Act.	 The French and Indian War takes place.	Parliament passes the Revenue, or Sugar Act.	Parliament passes the Quartering Act and the Stamp Act. Colonial delegates hold the Stamp Act Congress.

1778	1779	1780	1781	1783
 Cornwallis captures Savannah, Georgia.	John Paul Jones wins sea battle against the English in September.	Cornwallis captures Charleston, South Carolina.	The English surrender at the Battle of Yorktown and America wins the war.	The British and the Americans sign the Treaty of Paris.

at Yorktown

1767

Parliament passes the Townshend Acts.

1770

The Boston Massacre takes place.

1773

The Boston Tea Party takes place.

1774

The First Continental Congress meets in Philadelphia.

1775

APRIL 19 The Revolution begins at the Battle of Lexington and Concord.

MAY 10 The Second Continental Congress meets in Philadelphia.

1776

JANUARY 10 Thomas Paine publishes *Common Sense*.

JULY 4 The Declaration of Independence is endorsed.

1777

The Americans defeat the British at Saratoga on October 17; American troops spend the winter at Valley Forge.

1787

MAY 25 The Constitutional Convention meets.

SEPTEMBER 17 The Constitution is approved by the Convention.

1789

George Washington becomes the first U.S. president on April 30.

1790

Rhode Island is the last of the 13 states to ratify the Constitution.

1791

The Bill of Rights is approved and added to the Constitution.

To Find Out More

BOOKS

Ferrie, Richard. *The World Turned Upside Down: George Washington and the Battle of Yorktown*. New York: Holiday House, 1999.

Hudson, David L., Jr. *The Bill of Rights: The First Ten Amendments of the Constitution*. Berkeley Heights, NJ: Enslow Publishers, 2002.

Santella, Andrew. *The Boston Massacre*. Danbury, CT: Children's Press, 2004.

Waxman, Laura Hamilton. *An Uncommon Revolutionary: A Story About Thomas Paine*. Minneapolis, MN: Lerner Publications, 2003.

ONLINE SITES

Archiving Early America
http://www.earlyamerica.com

Kids in the House—The Office of the Clerk
http://clerkkids.house.gov/

Index

Bold numbers indicate illustrations.

About the Author

Melissa Whitcraft lives in Montclair, New Jersey, with her husband and their two sons. She has a Master of Arts in theater. In addition to plays and poetry, she has written both fiction and nonfiction for children. Her titles include *Tales from One Street Over*, a chapter book for early elementary grade readers. Her biography, *Francis Scott Key, a Gentleman of Maryland*, was published as a Franklin Watts First Book. Ms. Whitcraft wrote books on the Tigris and Euphrates, the Niagara, and the Hudson rivers for the Watts Library series. She also wrote *Seward's Folly*, *The Mayflower Compact*, and *Wall Street* for the Cornerstones of Freedom, Second Series.